The Little Book of Dylan™

First published 2005 by Boxtree
an imprint of Pan Macmillan Ltd
Pan Macmillan, 20 New Wharf Road, London N1 9RR
Basingstoke and Oxford
Associated companies throughout the world
www.panmacmillan.com

ISBN 0 7522 2522 7

Produced under license by Pathe Pictures Limited and Magic Rights Limited

© Magic Rights Limited/M.Danot 2005. The Magic Roundabout and all related titles, logos and characters are trademarks of Magic Rights Limited. Licensed by Magic Rights Limited. Based on the characters created by Serge Danot. All rights reserved.

Text © Pathe Pictures Limited. All rights reserved

Pathé Pictures presents in association with the UK Film Council and Pathé Renn, Pricel, France 2 Cinema and Canal + a Films Action / SPZ Entertainment/ bolexbrothers Production
THE MAGIC ROUNDABOUT
Tom Baker Jim Broadbent Joanna Lumley Ian McKellen Kylie Minogue Bill Nighy Robbie Williams Ray Winstone
Associate Producers Claude Gorsky Linda Marks Bruce Higham Andy Leighton Vertigo Productions
Based upon original characters created by Serge Danot with the participation of Martine Danot
Co Writers Raoff Sanoussi Stéphane Sanoussi
Screenplay by Paul Bassett Davies with additional material by Tad Safran
Executive Producers Francois Ivernel Cameron McCracken Jill Sinclair Jake Eberts
Producers Laurent Rodon Pascal Rodon
Directed By Jean Duval Frank Passingham Dave Borthwick
© Pathé Fund Limited 2004.

All rights reserved. No part of this publication may be reproduced, stored in or introduced into a retrieval system, or transmitted, in any form, or by any means (electronic, mechanical, photocopying, recording or otherwise) without the prior written permission of the publisher. Any person who does any unauthorized act in relation to this publication may be liable to criminal prosecution and civil claims for damages.

1 3 5 7 9 8 6 4 2

A CIP catalogue record for this book is available from the British Library.

Designed by seagulls

Printed by Proost, Belgium

The Little Book of Dylan

BOXTREE

'I know there's like, "no rest for the wicked", but I'm one of the good guys and right now I need a siesta.'

'Whoa man,
that is deep.'

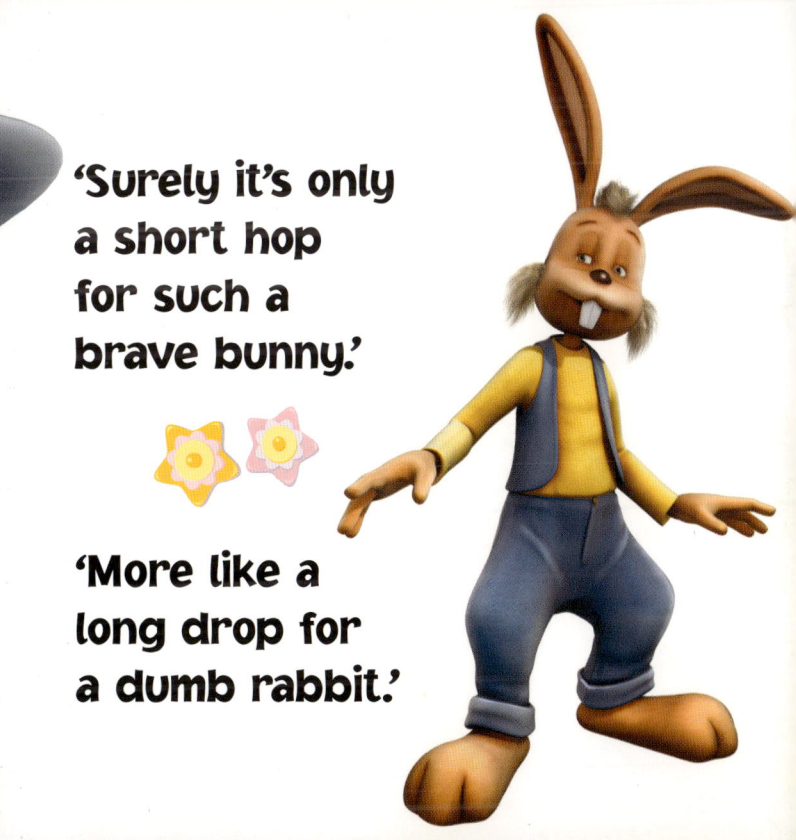

'Surely it's only a short hop for such a brave bunny.'

'More like a long drop for a dumb rabbit.'

'Man, they don't make crumbling rock causeways like they used to.'

'Cool light show, man.
Hello pretty lasers.'

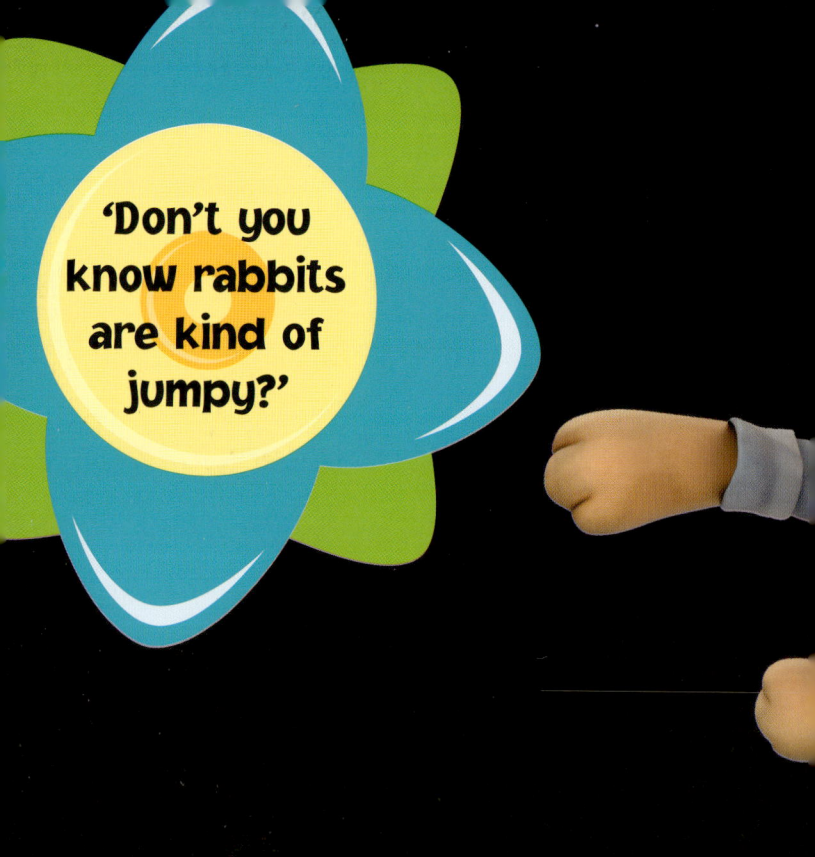

'Ooooff! You just don't know when you're beaten, do you? Take a chill pill, rabbit!'

'This guy is seriously messing with my karma.'

'Woah, that was some hit!'

'We should get some sleep, man.'

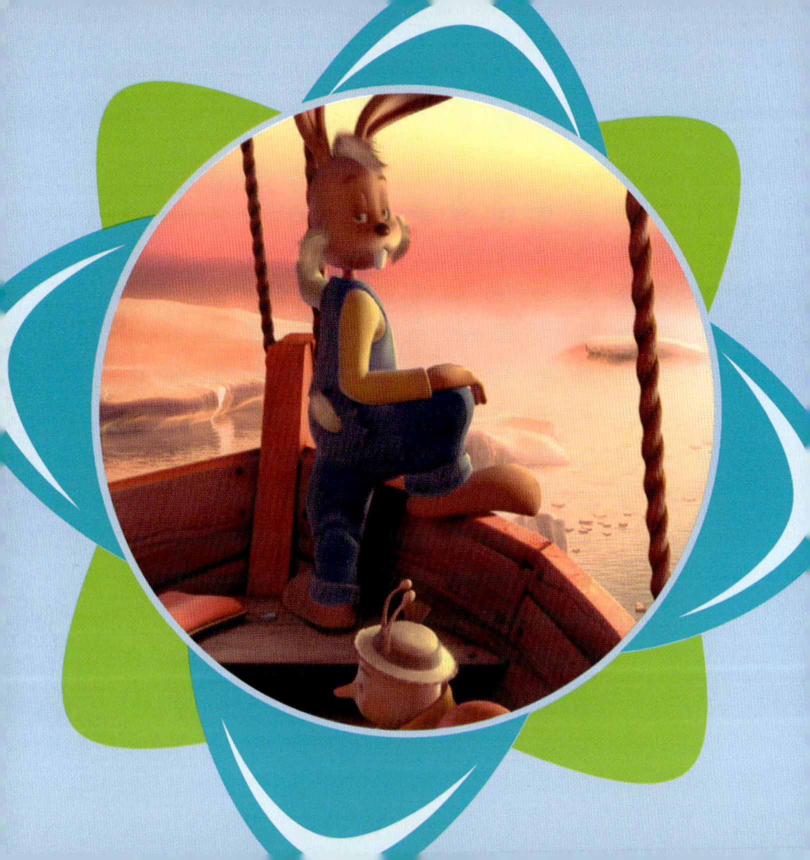

'Come on, people.
The sky's the
limit now!'

'Well done, Dylan. A balloon escape. My! You are clever.'

'It's all about altitude over attitude, Ermindude.'

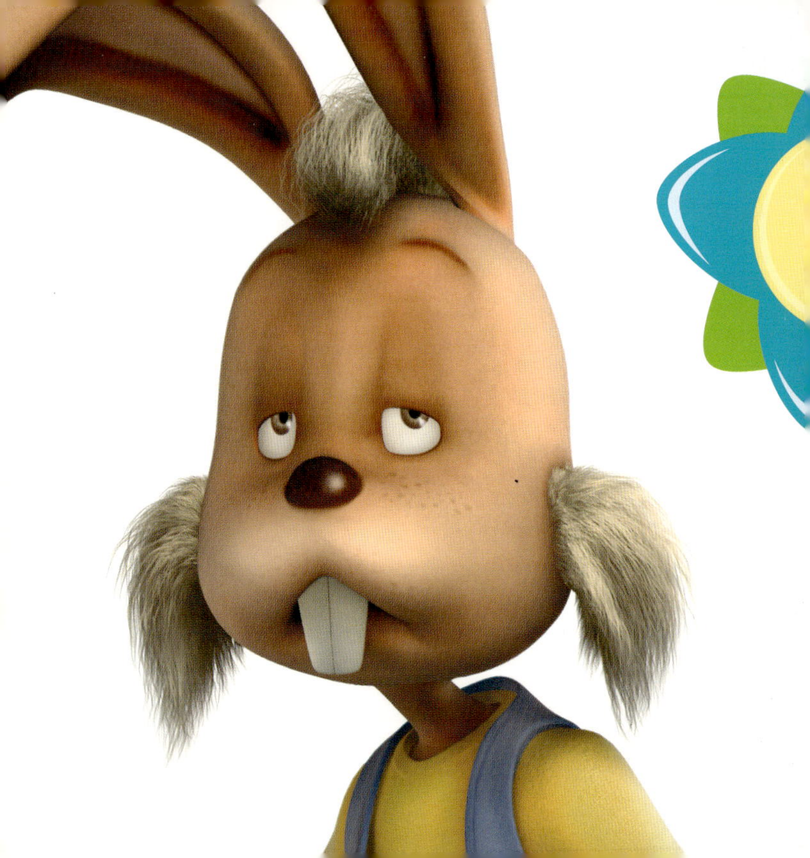

'So close and yet so far out!'

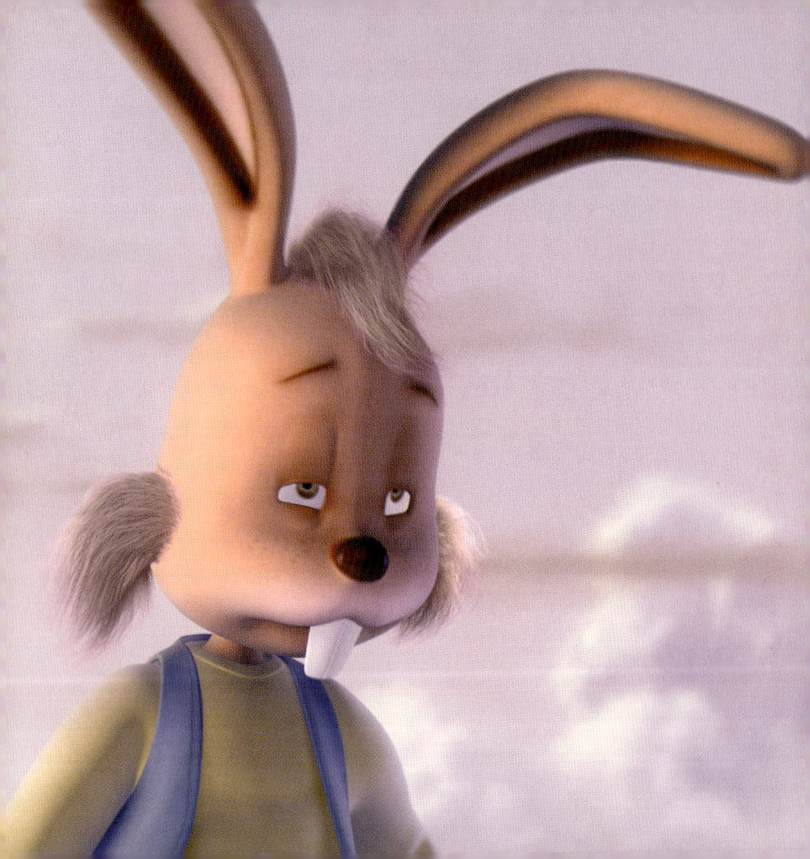

'Zeb's dead, baby, Zeb's dead.'

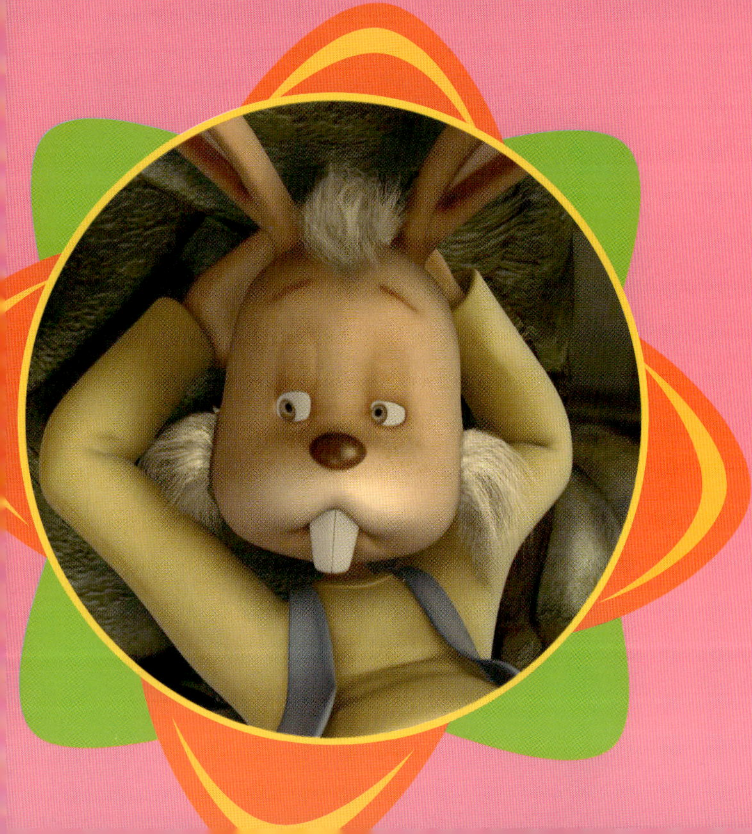

'But if it wasn't for time everything would, like, happen at once?'

'No way, man, I'm in a higher state of unconsciousness...'

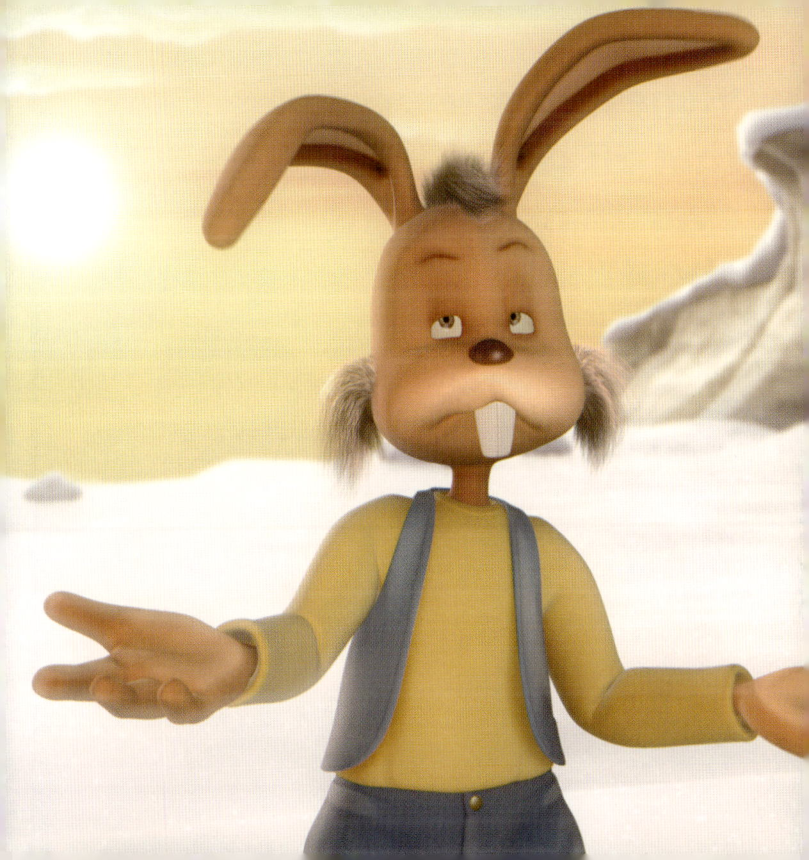

'Honestly, is that all you ever think about?'

'Sure. Whenever I'm awake.'

'Woah...
don't toast the
hamsters, dude...'